Other books by Nick Maslaney

How to Make Money From Rural Land Property

Option,
Sell,
and Create
Rural Land
Note Income

A Question and Answer Analysis
of Rural Land Owner Financing

Nick Maslaney

Option, Sell, and Create Rural Land Note Income: A Question and Answer Analysis of Rural Land Owner Financing © 2024 Nick Maslaney

Cover image: © Mare Kuliasz via iStockphoto
Cover & Book Design: Vladimir Verano, Vertvolta Design
Chapter photo: © Sveta Fedarava, via Unsplash.com
Edited by Jessica Levey

Published by Nick Maslaney
    Contact: land4all75@gmail.com
    Facebook: www.facebook.com: @nicholas.maslaney
    twitter.com: @NMaslaney

Print: 978-0-9981222-2-9
Ebook: 978-0-9981222-3-6
Audio book: 978-0-9981222-4-3

Contents

Introduction

If you ask an investor with no real estate experience what they think the best way to make money in real estate is, they might say income from single and multi-family rentals is the key to wealth. They'll tell you to buy single or multi-family housing and hold onto it forever. With the depreciation expenses for these types of properties, it's a no brainer. There's merit to these statements, and many people have done well with this oversimplified strategy.

Others will say that flipping homes is the key to wealth. In fact, many people watch television shows with people flipping homes successfully, and they have a real attachment to these programs and the personnel involved.

Not to diminish or marginalize these shows or this marketing strategy, but property flipping has increased at a feverish pitch, with no end in sight. Many real estate investors have done well and continue to do well with flipping homes. The problem with this strategy, however, is that you have to find another home or another piece of land to flip next, many times at a higher price, to continue the process.

There's a third way to generate income, create long term wealth, and serve your real estate clients, which is less known than the two strategies above. This method centers on earning a consistent monthly note income from rural land properties, and is the focus of this book.

Here's how it works: Part of this income is created as capital gain (hopefully) or capital loss (if applicable), and not rental income. A second part of the income is generated by interest; as interest is charged to the buyer, it's classified as interest and is collected by the seller as interest income. (Always consult with good tax professionals to understand how these transactions are taxed.)

The investor remains the financial owner of the property as the buyer becomes the legal owner. There's little management required (and in many cases none), and fewer hassles to deal with than there are with rental property. The end user of the property, not the investor, assumes the responsibility for management, maintenance, and upkeep of the property.

Many times, and for various reasons, this relationship also creates a better risk profile for an investor.

For example, when flipping houses, an investor buys low and hopefully sells higher. The risk profile for a flipper is 100% financial and legal conveyance to the buyer. However, the flipper eliminates cash flow from the discussion. A flipper usually has more capital gain taxes to pay, and, at times, these are short term capital gains. Short term capital gains are usually taxed at a higher rate than long term capital gains — real estate transactions that are held for longer than a year before selling.

The risk profile for note income also differs in many ways from that of any kind of real estate rental where day-by-day management is necessary.

Are there still risks in creating note income on owned real estate? Yes. This book will address those risks, along with other questions.

I decided to tackle this book about creating note income and cash flow through investing in real estate from a different perspective than others have.

Questions will comprise a big portion of the book. I'll give some examples, and the stories that I write are true. I'll still stay focused on basic principles, but will also try to cover more detailed ones as well.

I'll answer the most common questions that new investors ask, along with a few advanced questions. But if more questions occur to you, this is good. It can be frustrating to read a book involving investments, cash flow, and wealth creation, and then have more questions than answers, but if you do have new questions, contact me via email or on Facebook.

Chapter One

My Story: *Transactional and Relational*

Over thirty years ago, in September of 1991, I purchased my first real estate investment — a forty-acre property in rural Okanogan County, located in the north-central part of Washington State. I paid a $3,000 deposit and signed a lease option to purchase the property with a few hundred-dollar monthly payments. It was affordable, and I didn't think much of it at the time.

I'd arrived in the state only the month before, and was still active duty in the Navy. I wanted a piece of property in the middle of nowhere, and had met someone who had a lot of rural recreational property to sell.

It was a six-hour drive, one way, to reach the property. I didn't even own a car at the time, because owning one while living on a Naval ship wasn't convenient. After I purchased the property, I had to rent a car to reach it.

In my mind, this investment was purely transactional. But during the next thirteen months, my rural real estate hobby started to become more relational.

I called the realtor again and asked him if he had any other property to sell, and that I was looking to expand my holdings. He did, and told me about another forty-acre property available that bordered the first forty-acres I'd bought.

The common border between them was only one pin and one corner, and although they were on the same road, they looked very different. The second forty-acre piece had much more timber and better access, despite the pieces being only a few feet from each other.

A positive, which I didn't know at the time, was the timber value on the second property. I didn't know *anything* about timber values. The negatives were the time factor, and the fact that I'd have to make a cash offer. I had only three days to decide if I would buy, and needed $26,000 in cash.

It was a lot of money to buy rural land with no improvements. I made the long drive again over the weekend, visited my first property, and then looked at the new property.

On Monday morning, only three days after learning about the property being up for sale, I bought the second forty-acres for $26,000 cash, to close in thirty days. I'd sold some stocks for the cash, stocks that I had been buying since I was a paperboy at fifteen years of age.

I wondered if I was a genius or an idiot and a sucker.

Suddenly, I had eighty acres. I had never realized how much land that was. Where I grew up, in Aspinwall, a town in western Pennsylvania, an acre was a huge deal. Houses were built very close together, with one acre containing many homes. In the days following the purchase, my mind wandered, and I wondered what I was going to do with that much land!

My answer came in the most unusual way — and it was at this point that my new hobby started turning into a big interest, becoming more relational, and involving many other people.

At the time, the Northern Spotted Owl controversy was going wild. I'd never heard of a spotted owl where I grew up in western Pennsylvania. I used to only see cardinals, blue jays, and little finches. But the bird had just been declared endangered, and the Feds, along with some state governments, including Washington

State, moved to shut down or strictly limit any state or federally owned timber cutting near the spotted owl habitats.

The restrictions drove up demand, and anybody who owned any timber, in any fashion but especially private timber, was getting contacted to sell it — and I now owned a lot of timber.

One thing led to another, and I contacted the local mill owners to arrange for them to log my eighty acres.

There was just one problem. The first forty-acre property was not paid off in full, and according to the agreement, "no timber shall be removed until the property is paid off." I asked the realtor to talk to the 'big boss,' the owner of the big land company, to see if he would allow me to log the property if I used the proceeds to pay off the contract.

Now, remember, at this time I was only twenty-six years old, engaged to be married, and was still settling into life in a new state. Many of the people I interacted with, like those selling me property, logging the property, and arranging other things, were much older than me. In fact, some of them were old enough to be my parents.

I had to learn fast. I really had to fast track my understanding of the relational side of real estate investing to make this work.

It was not easy convincing. I gave the big boss my word that I would use all the timber proceeds to pay him off first, before I got anything. He told me that he didn't want me to clear cut it, and that I would have to leave a future timber harvest for the next property owner, mill owners, and loggers. (Little did I know at the time that *I* was the future harvester he was referring to —I ended up owning the land for many decades and I logged it again years later. I still own this property today, as of writing this book.)

I quickly understood that real estate *was* transactional, but it was also very relational. For me, this meant making the option land payments on time, not causing any problems for him, and being a good steward of the property.

I agreed, and he eventually allowed me to log the full eighty acres, with some reservations. In some ways, the transactional part led to a better payout, in the form of relational understandings. Concentrate on what you can, and the relational part evolves favorably.

Since I was a newbie at the time, starting a new business venture with new people, I didn't take anybody or anything for granted (Three decades later, I still don't take anybody or anything for granted.) I didn't know what the heck I was doing, and had to admit to having no knowledge about something I had a financial interest in. I had to rely on people who had more knowledge and experience than I did.

I oversaw the loggers on the property and gave them a wide latitude. It went well, and was very profitable. I got almost all my proceeds back from the timber sales, paid off the first forty-acre property to the big boss and his land development company, and kept a good chunk of the cash as profit. I was still in the Navy, and I was surprised that in that logging transaction, I made more money on those logs than I could make in one year of active duty.

I learned that it's ok to not be the smartest person in the room, or on a piece of property, when you start investing — there's no shame in this. It's a humbling and liberating process at the same time.

I reinvested those proceeds into another rural property in Spokane a few years later. And in 2002, after a few construction jobs, I was able to start a full-time business in rural land development and investment. I have now bought, developed, and sold many rural properties over the last thirty-plus years.

The shortest amount of time that I've held a property, from beginning to end, is fifteen months. I like to hold and receive long-term land contract payments on property, and I don't engage in intentional short-term flipping. I like to take time with my properties, including forming long-term relationships with clients.

Social and human capital becomes more important with long-term client building, and as the rural land properties get developed in the surrounding areas. I've had some properties over twenty years. In fact, I still own twenty acres of the original piece I bought in September of 1991, and the second forty-acre property I bought in 1992. These two properties continue to throw off income every month with satisfied customers.

This brings us back full circle with our discussion, on transactional versus relational aspects of investing.

Many times, flipping properties turns into a more transactional exercise and the relational side of real estate rural land investing is forgotten and ignored. If you invest in real estate for many years, you'll find yourself oscillating between these two areas of importance. Both are needed — transactional *and* relational. And both areas will always need to be improved.

You can't have one without the other.

Chapter Two

The Real Estate Industry

In general, the real estate industry has changed over many decades from a loose industry with many players to one with only a few big players. And the big players are only getting bigger. The profitable ones continue to become more profitable. The smaller, inefficient, inexperienced, and too-leveraged investors quit, become insolvent, and get bought out — as the bigger fish swallow the smaller ones.

An increasing number of online syndications continue to develop, especially large corporate ones, each with more money available and originating in many ways. In fact, REITs (real estate investment trusts) have become more influential and are making more money with less work than ever before, due to improved systems, increased financial and people leverage, and superior technological advantages.

With increased participation, cooperation, financial leverage, and competition in all areas of real estate investing — and among many more investors, speculators, and end users — the prices of all kinds of real estate have escalated quickly. As purchase prices go up, the rental prices for many apartments, homes, mobile homes with land, and rural undeveloped land follow, and have escalated to almost unsustainable levels.

As the cost of investing, owning, and holding rural land property increases, it's critical to have a strategy, or a group of strategies, to provide for yourself, your family, and your employees (if applicable), associates, and partners. Things change. Life happens, and you must adapt to the current conditions. People, including partners, buyers, and family, come and go.

As I wrote earlier, I'm a long-term investor. I think in terms of decades and longer. Yes, I started at the age of twenty six. It might be easy to say that then. Fast forward to 2023, and at the age of fifty eight, and I still think in terms of decades and longer. This approach worked in the past, and it continues to work well for me.

My business model has always been to make rural land buying simple, drama free, and affordable. The affordable part of the business model continues to be a challenge. I don't like to stretch my client's affordability comfort zone, so I will take less per month to keep long-term clients satisfied, to build long-term social relationships that translate into excellent social capital, and most importantly, to maintain consistent monthly cash flow.

I might be dead tomorrow, next week, or next year. What we build, develop, improve, and impart to others (especially to our friends and family) and to the land, will last for years after we leave this earth. What I write about now was true years ago, and will hopefully hold true in the future as well.

Chapter Three

Question and Answer Analysis Introduction

The following question-and-answer section composes a large portion of the book. All of the personal experiences I write about here *did* happen. There are many other stories that I could have included, but they're sensitive in nature and are best not disclosed. Still, these other experiences also help to inform this portion of the book.

The suggestions given here aren't one-size-fits-all, and in some circumstances and locations another answer could be better. For example, the properties and experiences I describe here all occurred in the state of Washington. I started writing this book while living in Washington, but finished it while living in another state, Florida, and have begun investing in rural land properties in the adjacent state of Alabama.

Many people who read this portion of the book might say that I should have done *this* or *that* instead. In fact, some really experienced real estate investors, and a few real estate lawyers, might say that they would never do what I've done when investing.

Successful real estate investing combines years of experience, good legal and moral representation, great mentorship, and, many times, a higher purpose that puts others before yourself.

For example, it might be legally acceptable to do something, but not morally acceptable. Conversely, something done on a land contract or property might be an acceptable moral action, but the law says something different. Which voice or action do we pursue?

While reading the following questions and answers, remember that many times, other options were considered, acted upon, and were not successful, or were advised against at the start. Many times, the option was the last or only available choice. Conversely, the given answer, action, or response to some of these questions was the first and only real choice — there were no other good choices.

Chapter Four

Questions: WHY?

1.   Why create rural land note income?

A. One of the main reasons to pursue this investment strategy is that seller-financed notes generate monthly income for the note holder. If the note holder (you, the seller) has a family, the family receives income as well. This monthly income can be used to pay bills, saved for other purchases, or reinvested in other properties.

In addition, seller-financed notes can be sold in the secondary market to raise cash.

B. Another reason to create note income becomes clear when the purchaser doesn't qualify for bank financing, which is quite frequently the issue. In this case, the seller might not want to be cashed out, and will want to have regular payments coming in every month instead.

This situation happened to me and my partner: My partner and I bought a ten-acre property many years ago on a seller-financed note. We then resold it on a seller note to another party on a 'wrap' — as in, wrapping a bigger note into a smaller note. What made this situation unique was the seller's situation; she was an elderly lady who wanted to receive a monthly payment for several years, in order to supplement her social security income for living expenses.

We agreed to her terms and paid the minimum each month, and for over five years, she had that note income from us to help her in her later years of life. She wrote a thank you letter to the escrow and note collection company when we finally paid it off.

Now, thirteen years later, my partner and I still have this property, throwing off income every month.

This example demonstrates that it's critical to listen to people's needs. *Listen* and then meet the needs of your clients. Try to create value and benefit for as many people as you can, every step of the way. This approach makes things go smoother and better results will occur.

C. In addition, a note seller might want to generate a second small stream of income. The note investor might have a full-time job, and won't want to spend much time on investments in the beginning. Two or three notes from seller-financed properties will allow a part-time investor to pay for their vehicle expenses, college tuition, or regular beach vacations — beach vacations which can help clear, replenish, and refocus the mind.

2. How do you grow a small note business into a larger one?

A. Establish a foundation: To go from a small note income on one or two properties to a larger income from many properties requires focus, discipline, and consistency.

First, I recommend having several properties paid off first, before using leverage. That's what worked for me, though that was several decades ago and the prices of real estate, including land, have escalated a lot the past thirty years. Everybody's situation is different.

I also like to start out with 'option to purchase' property agreements for reasons that will become clear in the examples below.

(Read a detailed description of this process in my first book, "How to Make Money from Rural Land Property".)

This process was developed over many years, in response to many experiences. When I started out selling properties on land contracts, it took time to learn the business. Unexpected things will happen. People make all kinds of plans, only to discover later on that those intentions were pipe dreams. Life happens, and those plans and ambitions cannot always be implemented. This is an unfortunate and harsh reality.

For example, you will encounter buyers who make a down payment, and then a few monthly payments, and then suddenly quit paying, without you ever hearing from them again. Sometimes they'll change their phone number, or the phone company cancels their service due to nonpayment.

In fact, many years ago, I had a strange situation happen to me: I had a rural property for sale that had an old mobile home located on the land. The mobile home was worthless, except for some valuable windows and scrap. It wasn't worth fixing up to live in.

I mentioned this in my ad and had a lengthy discussion about it with the buyer before they placed a down payment. I went above and beyond for full transparency, and stressed the need for long-term thinking.

Long story short, they put a down payment on the property and three weeks later I received a nasty email stating that they did not want to keep leasing the property because of the condition of the mobile home.

As another example, on the same property, I 'leased to purchase' to a couple who was living out of state. They made regular payments for about thirteen months, and then suddenly stopped making payments.

After the last payment, I got a call from a fraud investigator with the State, asking me about these two ex-clients of mine. I told the government officials what I knew about the couple, and that they had never lived in the state. I never heard back from the state investigators or my ex-clients again.

This is why I like to start out with 'option to purchase' property agreements.

Why? Because if a client cancels the option to purchase by not paying, or by leaving the area, then I don't have to spend money to forfeit or foreclose. In examples like the one above, there is zero cost of eviction, since they didn't occupy the property. (However, if the option buyer *does* occupy the property, quits paying, but will not leave the property, contact a good real estate lawyer in your state.)

If an option to purchase falls through, I can sell ('option to purchase') the property again with another agreement, to a better and more serious client.

After many other instances like the one described above during my first few years investing, I decided to build a good base of paid-off properties, and a few that produced a consistent cash flow every month.

B. Duplicate the formula: Once a few of my properties were paid off and I had cash flowing, I used that cash flow to pay for more of the same — I reinvested most of the income in similar properties, except for what I needed to cover a few necessary costs, like taxes.

For example, when I started to generate note income from several properties on a consistent basis, I used some of the note income to pay down the other properties I was buying. I had the note-processing company use the proceeds (assigned) to pay off my other notes as a buyer. This strategy resulted in increased net cash flow, from the underlying loans that were paid off.

In the beginning, you might want to have *at least* a 'three to one' ratio. That is, three contracts that are paid off, paying one loan. It's even better to have four or five contracts paid off, to pay for one loan.

As your experience grows along with your confidence, you can start adding on other properties, with more debt. Eventually you will have a 'five or six to three' or 'seven to four' ratio.

As more loans get paid off (either by bank loans, or by seller-financed loans, or 'wraps,' buying a property and selling to somebody on a higher payment) your cash flow will increase along with your borrowing capacity. There are various ways of using debt, including partnerships, seller financing, or wraps, and personal lines of credit, to expand your note income business and generate greater income.

To grow a small note income into a larger income, you must buy more properties, and have better income-producing properties, as well. I describe cash-outs in note seller financing in my first book (in Chapter 12) and it needs repeating here: If you get cashed out of a note-seller-financed property, you'll need a game plan to roll those funds into another investment or group of investments, to continue receiving a similar (or ideally, a higher) monthly income.

Here's an example: About fourteen years ago, I sold one of the first properties I'd purchased. At the time it was yielding no income per month. I used the cash proceeds from that sale to buy another property, which then began paying me $530 per month.

This $530 in income per month, accumulated over the past fourteen years, has enabled me to invest in other properties, pay needed expenses for my business, and to deploy funds to other places. To generate a larger monthly income, it takes the financial discipline to deploy cash-outs to higher income producing properties.

In summary, you can buy many of the same types of properties (small, medium, or large) to successfully grow from a small monthly income to a larger monthly income. This method is powerful because it duplicates a formula and system.

Second, use cash-outs from smaller properties or properties with no cash flow to buy properties that will produce a bigger monthly income. This can be done via 1031 exchanges or straight purchases of the cash-out properties, to resell.

Third, use 90% to 100% leverage to buy and resell (lease) on a wrap contract to another client.

3. What are the advantages of selling a property on a land contract?

There are many advantages for the seller when selling a property on a land contract.

Since you, the note holder, are a lienholder on the property, the maintenance, upkeep, and taxes become the responsibility of the buyer. Anybody who has previous experience with rental properties, or who currently maintains rentals, clearly understands this advantage. This translates to less overall work for you in both the short and long run.

Another benefit is that the seller terms, which dictate the amount of each monthly payment, the years of payout, and the date of each payment, are flexible. For example, a note can be written for five, ten, twenty, or thirty years. This is important, as affordability for the purchaser remains critically important for both the buyer and seller. I have personally created hundreds of notes on property owned in length from ten years, to thirty years, and everything in between.

Many years ago, a real estate agent arranged a sale for me to a married couple, on a land contract, and made sure that the monthly payment was affordable to them at the time. Then, after several years of making payments on the property, one of the partners died, and the monthly payment was no longer affordable. I reworked the note and made it even more affordable to the surviving spouse.

Affordability, accountability, and flexibility to my clients' ever-changing circumstances, plus the responsibility to meet those needs, are essential to my note business approach. This remains the DNA of my business mindset.

4. What are the advantages of buying a property on a note or land contract?

Note buyers see many of the same advantages as sellers. For the buyer, a flexible payment amount helps them to establish a homestead. Many times, private note terms are their only choice.

I have received and retained many clients who were in transition from personal financial crisis back to stability. Some of these clients were emerging from bankruptcy, or a nasty divorce, or from family struggles with deadbeat family members. A bank wouldn't lend to them, or even consider the risk. Frequently, people in these situations are very close to homelessness and despair. The struggle is real.

These examples demonstrate that real estate note income is not just about making money and cash flow. It's also about making a positive impact on individuals and their respective families. It's about helping people take the next positive step in their development.

For both note sellers and buyers, these opportunities create relationships that last for years, and at times, for life.

This strategy is all about long-term thinking, acting, and executing — which is antithetical to flipping properties and the transactional mindset of many real estate investors.

5. What is a 'note,' or what some people call a 'land contract'?

In general, a note creates a contractual financial and legal obligation between two people, a group of people, or a person and a company. This obligation between two or more parties dictates the responsibility, accountability, and legal remedies available for all parties.

Many conditions, expectations, and remedies create a legal note, and the language used to write one will vary from state to state. I will only mention a few of these situations here, so if you're not sure what your unique situation requires, contact a good legal resource for help.

So, what kind of language should be in each note? Although each state has its own laws as to what constitutes a legal and binding note, there are common items you'll need to include. Below are some of these particulars.

A. The specific parties involved in the note should be mentioned, specifically the buyer and seller. These parties must meet the requirements for legal consent and capacity to consent.

For example, if your state doesn't allow a minor to buy and sell a property, it would be advisable to not challenge state law. Selling to a minor might make the agreement unenforceable or render the note null and void.

As another example, if one of the parties to the note agreement has Alzheimer's, or is suspected of having it, it would be a good idea to have an addendum stating such. At the minimum, you'll want to contact a lawyer to check the legality of the agreement.

B. The note should include the amount financed, the interest rate (simple / compounded), the late fees incurred if a payment isn't made on time, and how many days past due will trigger a late fee. There should also be language about the prepayment of principal, and whether or not this is allowed.

C. Include the legal description of the property. This legal description should be specific and detailed. If the east corner of the property has only forty feet, for example, then that needs to be specified. Remember that many areas still use section, township, and ranges to give the legal description of properties.

D. Assignment of the note should be mentioned. If the note can be assigned, what are the conditions? If the note cannot be assigned, then strong, legal, concise and specific language needs to be written.

E. Who is servicing the note? Include these details. For example, is an escrow company receiving payments, or are the sellers receiving payments?

F. Are the taxes escrowed every month? They should be. Make sure the note payment includes an amount every month that will go towards paying property taxes. This helps buyers, and especially sellers, because if note payments aren't being made, it usually means that tax payments to the county aren't being made either.

As an example: Many years ago, my partner and I purchased a property and then sold it on a land contract. When we forfeited the buyer after eight months of nonpayment, we had to pay over $4,000 in back taxes, in addition to the legal costs. The buyers had already left the area and moved a few states away!

Ensuring that a portion of the monthly payment goes toward property taxes will do wonders for your peace of mind, in addition to your cash flow.

G. Details about who will pay the note collection fee every month should be included as well. Many people think incorrectly that the seller should bear all the note collection costs. Others believe that the buyer should pay all the note collection costs. And a good majority believe that the note collection costs should be split evenly between seller and buyer, since it's in the best interest of both to have a neutral party servicing the note.

This fee can be negotiated between the buyer and seller. However, one word of caution must be included here: Since the note collection fee will increase over time, it matters greatly how the original agreement was created. What starts out as a small fee can become much bigger over time. From personal experience, I have seen fees on a seller-financed note *double* over eight to ten years. This amount really adds up over time.

There are many other things that need to be included in the note. If in doubt, contact a good real estate lawyer that specializes in this area of real estate.

6. What if they don't pay?

People ask me on a regular basis, 'What if a buyer doesn't pay?' This is a complicated question. In fact, I could easily write another book about just this one question, and the many ramifications of nonpayment. To complicate things even more, state and federal laws have changed a lot over the past three years, with COVID-19 on everyone's radar.

Now, in my first book, I discuss the three best outcomes of selling a property on a land contract. These outcomes must be kept in mind when considering questions of nonpayment, as they represent the ideal endgame, completion, or transition of your investment:

1. Buyers pay the property off in a short time, maybe in two to five years.

2. A buyer gets behind and quitclaims the property back to the seller, or the seller forfeits from a legal action. In this outcome, the property reverts to the seller.

3. The buyer goes the full term, or even longer, and pays the note off.

With these goals in mind, let's get back to the question of "What if they don't pay?"

The first piece of advice I can give is that nonpayment *happens*. Buyers will quit paying at various points during the duration of a contract. If you want to build a portfolio of land contracts, you'll have to get used to it. It happens.

The second piece of advice I have to offer is to *be patient*. Patience is needed to navigate, negotiate, and eventually resolve issues of nonpayment. For example, patience will help you determine if payments will continue in the future, or, if they will not, how to get the buyer to quitclaim the property back to you. This type of situation demands caution, and therefore patience.

This leads to a third piece of advice, which is to have a good real estate lawyer handle these types of legal actions. For example, a quitclaim deed doesn't guarantee much of anything. And if the buyer has personal liens, or encumbers the property to another legal agreement or creates a problem on the property, then a forfeiture or foreclosure might be needed to eliminate other liens junior to the land contract of the seller. A good lawyer will know the best way to proceed.

Let me give a personal example: A couple purchased a property from me on a land contract many years ago. They paid faithfully every month, on time, for several years. Then, they got six months behind and I had a hard time reaching them. I emailed, called, and texted, but did not get any response.

The buyer finally made all six past-due payments without an explanation, plus the late fees, to bring the property current. Then, a few months later, payments stopped again. They were three more months behind when they finally called me.

They told me that they'd moved, apologized for being late again, and said they were no longer interested in the property or in paying for it. I asked if I could help them list it with an agent so that they could make money on it, but they declined and agreed to quitclaim the property back to me instead.

I saved thousands of dollars on forfeiture costs, sold the same property again on a land contract shortly afterward, and was able to continue receiving monthly income on the property again quickly. Patience paid off!

Here's another example: Many years ago, on another property, a buyer quit paying. He was several months behind, and it was not looking good for him. I was close to forfeiting the contract to get the property back, because he wouldn't respond to my letters, phone calls, or other attempts to contact him.

Then, I got a phone call from his mother. She apologized to me about her son's missed payments and told me that he'd died of an aggressive type of cancer. "What can we do?" she asked.

I told her that I would not forfeit, even though I had every legal right to, and gave her the phone number of a real estate agent who could help her sell the property. I also told her that I was sorry for her loss, and that I thought her son was a great guy and that we'd seemed to really connect on a deeper level than just 'buyer and seller.'

The real estate agent sold the property, I got cashed out of the contract, and my deceased client's family was able to get something back financially following his loss.

The lesson here is again one of *patience*. Don't jump to any conclusions about anybody. It does nobody any good. Whatever preconceived notions you might have about why somebody isn't paying, those beliefs are usually wrong.

Once again, patience, understanding, and peaceful persistence guarantees the best results.

7. What's the best way to handle late payments, or inconsistent payments?

This question is similar to the one above, but deals with a responsive payer who 'gets behind' on the note, or isn't current on their note payments. If you sell property on a land contract, this experience *will* occur. Though it's easier said than done, extreme patience in these cases will lead to better outcomes for all.

There are three main types of payers on real estate contracts:

1. There are the 'on-time payers,' those who pay on time every month regardless of any personal issues. I have had, and still have, many of these types of payers.

2. The second type of payer is what many call a 'late payer.' These payers pay on a regular basis, but the payments are usually late.

   For this type of payer, the key is to keep them current as often and for as long as possible. Most of the time, late payers stay current, and soft and subtle reminders like an email or a letter work well. But sometimes, the 'late payer' turns into a 'slow payer.'

3. The third kind of payer is the 'slow payer.'

   The slow payers will drive anybody in this business crazy, leaving you dizzy and confused. Banks and long term note investors will tell you that nothing drives them crazy like a slow payer.

   What describes the payment behavior of a slow payer? Many times, the slow payer starts out as a good, on-time payer. They'll pay on time for many months, and even years. Then, they get behind one month, catch up for a few months, fall behind another two months, and catch up to only one month behind again.

While this cycle goes on and on, you'll feel like you're on an out-of-control roller coaster ride that never stops. The ride was fun in the beginning, but over time you wonder when it will stop (with forfeiture or foreclosure action), become a smooth ride again (returning to on-time payments), or settle into something in between.

Of all the note collection business nuances, this is the most difficult one for me to manage. Even after a few decades of experience, this is true. However, I have learned to live with this occurrence.

Here's a personal example: Many years ago, I had a client who followed this exact type of transition, from 'on-time payer,' to 'late payer,' to 'slow payer.' It was a strange occurrence for me at the time, since I had little experience in the business then. Even more odd, I thought, was that it was one of my smallest monthly note payment amounts.

My client eventually got over six months behind, with no payments, not even late payments, coming in. It was several years into the note cycle, which meant that the property was very valuable. The client had completely developed the property with his own money (adding water, power, phone, and septic to the land), and the property was now worth over ten times the value it had been when I bought it.

Since the circumstance involved many of my client's family members, I was determined to resolve the issue beneficially for all. I was also determined to keep him on the property, and to not foreclose on it.

Long story short, and after some serious negotiating tactics, the client finally brought the account current. I found out from another of my client's family members that he hadn't known he was behind the entire time! He eventually paid me off and cashed me out of the contract.

It was a good lesson to learn. It takes much patience to handle these types of accounts and various client's relationship dynamics.

8. How long should a note seller wait to get paid before starting the forfeiture process?

Many people who read this might ask how long a note seller should wait to get paid. At what point do note sellers start the forfeiture process? Is there a set time limit, like three, four, or six months?

The only way I can answer these types of questions, after more than three decades of experience and exposure to the land contract business, is to say: There is no right or wrong answer. What might work for some people might not work for others.

For me, it comes down to my personal business model approach of long-term thinking. I want clients who last for life, or at least for many decades. Ok, so I might not live for many more decades, or even one more, but I want how I treat people to be remembered for decades, and shared in stories with their family members.

When people need help, instruction, guidance, or leadership in the worst way, emotional intelligence is essential. This means relating, understanding, and identifying ways to be helpful. Your emotional intelligence must be elevated, to many times higher than any profit-driven, zero-sum, winner-takes-all business mentality.

Don't get me wrong: The note business is a *business*. One must treat it like such. But there will always be clients with personal issues, stories, and struggles to navigate as well.

9.   What are late fees?

Late fees are assessed to a purchaser of a property if a scheduled payment is not received on time, or is late beyond a set period of days (a grace period).

When I first started in the note business, I allowed a generous grace period before charging late fees. But after several years, I discovered that I had to shorten this grace period. A note seller's goal is to get regular payments on time: This creates consistency, predictability, and accountability, and good cash flow metrics. When I shortened the grace period, client payments became more predictable and consistent.

I also discovered that if the note is still early in the seasoning (within two years of purchase), that it's best to be prompt, courteous, and firm with a note buyer whenever a payment is late. I've seen note buyers make late payments within the first six months of purchase because they believe it's a normal thing to do.

In these cases, I send multiple kinds of correspondence to make sure a buyer understands that this thinking is wrong, and that late payments are not acceptable. It's vital to notify clients about the importance of prompt payments early on. This shows professionalism. If the note buyer thinks that you don't care about the payments, they might decide to pay you whenever they want.

10. What happens if a note buyer declares bankruptcy during the payment period?

Bankruptcy is a legal process that is at times varied and specific, and can happen for many reasons. There are several different types of bankruptcy declarations and remedies. Many times, a client declaring bankruptcy will want to keep the land, as well as a home if one is there, especially if they've been paying on the note for years.

As with any legal process in real estate, lawyers will become involved. And when lawyers become involved, it's imperative that you have good legal help on your side. Federal and state-specific laws will determine the direction of the legal process. If you're not sure what effect a client's bankruptcy will have on the real estate note, consult with a good real estate lawyer to protect your interest. Usually, a note seller or note holder is not involved in the client's legal details, unless they are mentioned in the legal description of the proceedings.

Personally, I've had several buyers declare bankruptcy during the payment period on a private land contract. Most of the time, the process resulted in a favorable outcome for both me and the buyer.

11. What kind of income is note seller income?

The usual disclaimer in this section remains true: Get good accounting and legal help from experts who understand the tax laws applying to note seller income. These accounting professionals should also understand any recapture and basis costs that occur when a property is sold several times over the years.

There are two types of income generated by selling property on a contract, deed of trust, or any other financial obligation. These are capital gains (or losses), and interest income (which will depend on the rate of interest and other factors).

When a note seller, or any real estate investor, sells a property via a land contract, deed of trust, or other promissory financial obligation, it creates a tax liability for them. The extent of this liability depends on many circumstances. Without getting too in depth about the legal aspects and tax consequences of note selling, I will say that it's critical to keep good records, and to have a good accountant who understands this area of tax law.

For example, the cost of the property (or as accountants will call it, the 'basis') can change over time, based on many factors. If you resell the property several times, spend money on legal costs or improvement costs, or incur other costs associated with basis adjustment, these will all affect the tax liability you owe.

If the property is held longer than one year, capital gain income is taxed as a long-term capital gain rate, which is usually more favorable than a short term rate. If the property is held less than one year, this income is considered a short-term gain and taxed differently, usually at a higher rate (depending on your personal tax rate).

12. Is the note business scalable, residual, and leverageable?

The answer to these three questions is *yes*.

A. Let's take the question of scalability first. How can the note business be scalable?

Scalability requires duplication. It will demand much time from you in the beginning, in order for you to learn a certain type of investment model and duplicate it. There will be mistakes and false starts. Start with one approach, copy that model, and apply it again and again. One property becomes two. Two becomes three, and four, and so on.

Anytime scalability is being considered, the biggest issue is often how to choose those one or two properties to start the process. I recommend starting with something specific. This might be how much money, or what percentage, you allow for a downpayment. It might be only investing in a specific property type. For example, you might want to start by investing in only rural highway properties, or you might want to deal only with improved properties. Or, it might be something else.

Once you have one, two, or three properties that meet your criteria, and are making payments of them every month, you can scale that model to other areas, whether locally, regionally, or many time zones away.

Also, at some point, moving from a part-time to a full-time commitment becomes necessary. The more properties you have that generate note income, the greater the opportunity to turn your business into a full-time income, with a more regular time commitment.

B. Now let's look at the residual question. 'Residual income' means ongoing cash flow, with very little additional work.

Is the note business a residual business with residual income? Yes, this business is a residual income opportunity. In fact, this aspect is one of the biggest advantages of this type of real estate investing.

Consider that most real estate agents work for commissions. They make a sale, collect a commission, and repeat the process. No sales means no commissions and no income. But when a real estate investor sells a property by creating a note, the income becomes residual for however long the buyer pays on the note. Month after month, the payments keep arriving.

I've received payments on some properties for over ten years. In fact, I have several long term clients who have been paying for over twelve years on the same properties. Some clients I've had for over fifteen years, involved with several different properties. These clients start with one property, paying on it for a few years, and then their situation changes and they need something different. So I found them a better property, one that fit their new needs, and they continued to make monthly payments on these new properties. (Remember, if you don't solve your client's needs, your competition will.)

This is a lot of residual income month after month. I've gone on vacations, attended weddings and funerals, become sick, and funded family visits with the multiple residual-note income streams that hit my checking and savings account each month, despite not being in the area. Often, I'm several states and time zones away from the properties in question.

This residual income really became important during COVID-19. During the period of lockdowns and restrictions, my partner and I were still getting payments on most of our properties. In fact, we even completed a small logging operation on one of our properties during this time. We received money from the timber, and some locals got some firewood to use from the operation.

C. Last, let's look at the question of whether or not the note business is leverageable.

Yes. Leverage can be used to increase your business income, but it must be used cautiously. I personally implement the 'long game' of leverage. Now, I'm not suggesting all people use this style, and people must find their own style that works. Still, it's worth noting that I owned several properties, free and clear and throwing off income every month, before I started using the 'OPM' game (Other People's Money game), including bank money, lines of credit, and wraps.

Leverage exists in many forms. Three of these types are financial leverage, people leverage, and skill leverage. For example, below we discuss one important type of leverage — financial leverage.

Financial leverage happens when money is borrowed from a bank, a person, or from another financial entity. Money exists everywhere. Many financiers want to lend money to people. It's critical when borrowing money from anybody to understand the terms of repayment. You'll want to know: Is there an acceleration clause attached to the loan? Does the lender want the option to call the loan whenever a crisis happens at home, in another country, or at their company?

When using financial leverage for wraps (buying a property and selling to somebody on a higher payment), it's vital to understand the financing terms completely. The last thing a note investor wants to do is have a note called when they are receiving payments on a property with borrowed or leveraged funds.

Therefore, a line of credit at a bank can be better at times, but not always. After all, a line of credit is ongoing.

A word of caution on lines of credit: Lines of credit can be pulled. I took my note business full time in late 2002 and used lines of credit several times, and it really helped. But in mid-to-late 2006 through 2008, when the banks froze lending to smaller investors, including myself, our line of credit was canceled. They didn't demand a full repayment, but it stopped me from taking any more money.

Luckily, it didn't matter, because in a period of five years, my business was self-funding, and I didn't need any money from banks. In fact, some of the same banks who had denied me for an initial line of credit folded, and were no longer in business. Some banks got purchased from stronger banks who were more responsible with their lending. It was an amazing thing to witness and become part of a historical moment.

Eventually, I had private funds with other investors, and my cash reserve was sufficient. The end goal is to become self-funding, as well as to access private funds from lenders who understand the business. These private investors know that the note business remains a long game.

13. What is the difference between negotiating, haggling, and bartering?

Many times, the terms 'negotiating,' 'haggling,' and 'bartering,' are used interchangeably, like they mean the same thing or have the same result when used. But this is incorrect. Negotiating does not mean the same thing as haggling or bartering.

A. Negotiating is best defined as getting both parties to agree to something while each party gets something that benefits them. Each gets something they didn't have before the process started. Negotiating improves, clarifies, and delivers value to everybody.

    For example, offering a seller $2,000 less on a rural land property that was listed for $20,000 dollars, but is really worth $30,000 dollars, does not imply good negotiating skills. In addition, losing a purchase to a competitor for offering $3,000 less, because your competitor understood the property's true worth, is not good negotiating or sharp business skills.

    However, convincing a seller to accept a seller-financed note with a small down payment so that you can wrap a smaller note (of their land payment) with a bigger one (that you've already agreed to with *your* buyer), implies good negotiating skills.

B. Bartering is best defined as a give and take relationship. For example, a seller might need a $500 land payment in order to pay an underlying smaller payment of $300, while the buyer needs the expertise of the seller to install a septic system. Or maybe the buyer is short of cash, and needs $5,000 cash to install a septic system, but can still comfortably make the $500 land payment. Bartering and negotiating can go together many times.

C. Haggling usually means agreeing to something, but each party tries to meet the other party's specific number. Many people get distracted in haggling and lose sight of the bigger and smaller pictures of negotiating and bartering. Haggling is overrated, while negotiating is underestimated.

Here's a personal example: Many years ago, my partner and I purchased two adjacent rural land properties that were completely undeveloped. They ran north to south, totaling a little over nine acres. The north lot, that was on the highway, was around 4.6 acres, and the adjacent southern lot was roughly 4.41 acres. The offering price on both lots was $25,000.

I really wanted this property, and I knew it was a good deal even at full price. I wrote the homeowner a personal letter before he listed it with an agent, but he didn't respond, and three months later he listed the property.

A local buyer offered him $500 less than the full asking price. That buyer might have thought that it was smart to haggle with him, to get a deal on the land. But we knew what it was worth, and offered full price — the full $25,000 — and closed in less than thirty days.

Fifteen years later, that property has been a real money maker. One of the lots got completely developed, with a local family really enjoying living there, making affordable monthly payments that we receive as monthly income. (Remember, real estate isn't just about making money; it is also about providing housing at an affordable price.)

14. Are there people who do not, cannot, or will not negotiate?

If you would have asked me this question during my first ten years in the note creation business, I would have answered a firm *no*. And in my over thirty years of experience investing in real estate, with twenty-plus years as a full-time investor, I've found that the percentage of people who will not negotiate honorably, or who will not adhere to the rule of law, is very small. I calculate it as less than ten percent of people.

However, as the rule of law, property rights, and legal, financial, and historical jurisprudence breaks down, collective negotiating between people breaks down as well. In other words, people get what they can, and forget about others in the process.

This question is relevant in many areas of real estate investing, including the note business. People who will not negotiate usually have a breakdown in some area that prohibits them from thinking clearly. It could be a lack of respect for somebody or something. It might be self-righteousness, self-absorption, or self-importance that rules the day. People get full of themselves and overestimate their knowledge, and forget they can be wrong, *are* wrong, or that they'll lose everything if they don't take a step back from things.

For example, many years ago, I sold a property to a client who caught the self-righteousness bug. He, as many others do, felt that he could buy a property and forget about everybody and everything else involved — including neighbors, rule of law, and decades of property law governing roads and prescriptive easements.

I'll summarize the ten- plus years that followed into a few paragraphs: The client bought the property from me, and for years used the same road that all the surrounding neighbors used to get to their properties. This road went through his property, and he knew that the road was considered a legal easement for all of the other property owners. It was even recorded as such on all of his local neighbors' property deeds. In fact, I personally used this road for years before selling him the property, and I disclosed this to him as well when he made the purchase.

But a few years later, he got into a petty disagreement with his neighbor and tried to prevent the neighbor from using the road to access the new home he'd built. Soon after, he tried to prevent *all* of his neighbors from using the road.

This client started a war with all of us that he could not, would not, and did not win. In court, the judge asked him which road he was using to get to his property. It was an awkward moment when he admitted that he was using the same road that he was trying to prevent everybody else from using.

After this disagreement, the client quit paying me, and after ten-plus years of option and contract payments, I forfeited him out and took the property back again. Within a few months, I'd sold the property to somebody else.

The moral of the story translates to this: Self-righteousness and self-absorption gets nobody anywhere. It will, and it does, become an expensive lesson.

15. Is there such a thing as an ideal client from a note seller's perspective?

Many people have asked me this question over the years: What would a note seller's ideal buyer look like, if such an ideal exists? The best answer to this question hinges on many different factors, some of which might be unexpected.

For example, some of my best, consistent note payers — clients with no late fees, who made payments on time for many years — began with horrible credit scores. These clients were irresponsible in the past, but became excellent neighbors within their communities. They understood what it was like to start over. They didn't take anybody or anything for granted. They had a sense of purpose, a renewed sense of identity, and a positive outlook that was contagious to those around them.

Conversely, I once had a client with a high net worth, making an excellent income, and with a great personal reputation, who made only ten option payments before defaulting and giving me back the property without any expensive legal action. Although he could have easily paid off the property, his health and personal issues prevented him from making any more payments.

In another example, two clients, a married couple, paid responsibly on their land contract for four years before they suddenly quit paying. They quitclaimed the property back to me, and I resold it five months later. I later found out that they'd divorced, and that the last thing they wanted to deal with or fight about was the land and the monthly payment, even though they both had very good jobs and one of them could have easily afforded the land payment on their own.

These examples demonstrate that people and their behaviors don't always align with our expectations. In short, don't stereotype, discriminate, or assume anything about people — good or bad — when it comes to whether they'll make their land payments. Each note seller must determine their own system for evaluating credit worthiness, and your system might not match up with other people's ideas or conventional thinking.

16. What are second generation land sales?

When you sell land to the children of former clients (so, selling land to both adult children and their parents), this is called a 'second generation land sale.' You might have sold the parents the same property, or a different property. If you participate in the note business for long enough, say for several decades, and treat the business in a long-term fashion, you could and *should* experience second generation land sales.

As with many areas of the note business, especially rural land notes, no guarantees exist. You might think you have a good relationship with the parents, and that the note experience was good, but your experience might not be the same with their kids. Kids, as a later generation, bring in different viewpoints. And these kids have heard about you from their parents and friends, after all, rural small towns talk, and that talk gets around.

I've had several experiences with second generation land sales over the years. I don't treat the second generation any differently than I did the first one. I continued with the same business model, which is built on long-term thinking, and with people, the property, and the consistent application of fairness for all and its center.

It's important to note that many people in these second generations have wanted special favors because of my previous relationships with their parents. As an example, one elderly client died suddenly, and passed the property and note responsibilities to his children. They almost lost the property by getting very far behind (over five months behind).

During that time, I thought of their father, with whom I'd had a really good relationship. We'd had a special relationship that transcended the transactional aspects of note buyer and seller. I didn't treat that note any differently, because I thought very highly of, and really respected, their father, and eventually they brought the payments current.

I give many others time to catch up on their payments as well. In fact, even if I didn't like a client's children, I would still give them more than enough time to catch up on late payments.

This brings up a very important point that should be mentioned: Don't ever let your feelings about someone dictate your business model, or affect how you treat a specific account. Leave your personal feelings out of business dealings. We had a saying in the Naval corrections field that I served with for three years, which went like this: "Fair, firm, and impartial rules the day, night, and all year long." I try to apply this principle with everybody all of the time.

I've also had a few experiences selling to second generation in-laws, such as sons or daughters-in-law. The same approach described above applies here, as well. Many times, in my experience, the parents can't make their payments and their daughter-in-law or son-in-law will step in and step up to take over. Often a forfeiture action takes place to clear out the old liens. Frequently, these children-in-law are occupying the property and helping with their spouses' parents in various ways. They may have small children. The last thing they want to do is get evicted from the property because their parents-in-law can't pay the note.

In these situations, work out a deal with the son or daughter-in-law so that they can stay on the property and you, as a note seller, continue to receive monthly payments. This requires talking, cooperating, and listening. It's a win-win for all involved.

Once again, my advice is to leave your personal feelings about the parents, however positive or horrible they might be, out of the business end of things. Second generation sales translate into longer note payments for you, fewer evictions for the families, continuity for other family members, and an improved business reputation for the note owner (*you*, if you're the note seller).

17. What is the difference between quitclaim deeds, warranty deeds, or deeds of trust?

First, these terms are legal classifications. I will caution again that the best way to understand these terms fully is through the use of competent real estate legal counsel.

I've bought and sold many properties over the past three decades using all three of these legal terms — quitclaim deeds, warranty deeds, and deeds of trust. I'll try to generalize the first two of these in the context of real estate:

A. Quitclaim deeds: A quitclaim deed guarantees absolutely nothing. When a seller quitclaims a property to a buyer, the buyer assumes 100% of the risk, including any liens of the seller, property liens, or actions pending against the property during or after the transfer.

Quitclaim deeds can be used by governments, investors, or private parties during tax sales. Quitclaim deeds are used by parties in lieu of foreclosure and forfeiture in order to avoid a long, arduous, and expensive legal procedure to get the property back to the seller(s). Quitclaim deeds can also be used to transfer property from one family member to another. I've used quit-claim deeds many times in the past three decades. Some of my best deals as a buyer utilized quitclaim deeds.

Quitclaim deeds have their danger and their usefulness at the same time. It's imperative to understand these types of legal documents and the risks associated with them.

B. Warranty deeds: A warranty deed is another type of deed buyers and sellers commonly use. In fact, this deed might be the most common one. It's generally used when realtors are involved, when dealing with experienced real estate investors, and in various other real estate transactions.

Since a lot of real estate transactions occur with the help of realtors, it might be safe to say that most real estate sales involve a warranty deed, or some variation of one.

A warranty deed states that the seller guarantees a clear title, along with any disclosures, or that a title will be cleared and paid before closing date. Another way of saying this is that the seller guarantees a free and clear title, except for what is recorded on the title report. It's up to the buyer to accept the title, as disclosed by the seller and title officer (some might use the term 'title abstract').

C. Deeds of Trust: In a Deed of Trust, there are usually three people involved. The third person is the trustee, and this person will hold the title to the property. Deeds of Trust are different from warranty or quitclaim deeds.

One of the first things that might appear on a title report are local property taxes. These taxes, if delinquent, will appear as a lien against the property. Closers that are any good at their job will make sure that any taxes owed get paid before or during the closing process. If they don't, the buyer will have a new lien, and an obligation to pay. Other liens that might appear on a title report consist of unpaid child support, unpaid tickets, and alimony.

This matter of liens complicates many things. It's vital to understand the lien process, or to have good legal help if you don't.

18. What is the title company's responsibility regarding the disclosure of liens on property?

A good question, raised by the discussion above, is what a title company's responsibility is regarding the disclosure of liens on property.

In my first book, I discuss title reports in detail, but to keep it short here: The title company discloses the title report. It's only a report. The word guarantee should not be mentioned. Except in rare instances of fraud, title companies are generally untouchable because they 'except,' meaning they don't include coverage and escape liability, more things than they cover.

Read a title report and you will see that they 'except' themselves out of *almost everything*, including the time of day. Many title officers and title company employees might agree with this, and many might disagree. But either way, title reports are produced with many layers of insurance.

Many times, the company insuring such things doesn't reside in the area of the property. In fact, they might only have a local office that services the local area, while the business itself is based many states or time zones away.

19. What are some of the biggest risks or concerns for the seller of seller-financed rural land property?

Many risks exist for the seller. Here are three of the most important risks to consider:

A. Nonpayment: The biggest risk is nonpayment of note payments. Although I mentioned this concern and the potential outcomes of nonpayment in another question, it's important to discuss it again. To explore the risk of nonpayment, let's review the the two basic ways to originate a loan from seller financing, and weigh the risks of each:

1. Some people will make a small, medium, or big down payment on the property and finance the rest on a short, medium, or long-term seller-financed note.

2. Other people will write up a 'lease to purchase' or 'option' agreement. They'll collect monthly payments, and apply all or a portion of those payments to the down payment. A lease to purchase or option term can last for six to nine months, or for several years, depending on the agreement made.

After so many years working in the note business, I have a lot of experience with both methods, and still use both when offering seller financing on a property. There are advantages and disadvantages to both of these methods.

The main advantage of a big down payment is that you get a lot of money up front. This provides security in the case of nonpayment early or later in the note financing period.

The main disadvantage of a big upfront down payment is that your buyer won't demonstrate much of a payment history, the way they would if you sold it on a twelve or twenty-four-month lease or option to purchase agreement. In those types of agreements, a seller is able to see exactly how the buyer pays. For example, does the buyer pay early, on time, or are they always late with a payment?

Some of the best note payers I've had on seller-financed agreements have been those making a small down payment or no down payment. Instead, I offered a lease or option to purchase agreement over a period of one to three years, and I got to see how they paid. Then, when we closed out the lease to purchase agreement, and the document became a land contract, they continued paying on time, all the time.

These long-term clients understood the process, and knew they were investing in their personal and family's future. This method is not for everybody.

Conversely, I've also had good success with clients who made medium and large down payments. These clients had the money upfront, understood the agreement, and paid on time, all the time, even with no payment history.

Nevertheless, I've had clients not pay or quit paying regardless of the method used. Any seller-financed note comes with a risk of nonpayment.

B. Actions and behaviors of land buyers: I've sold many properties, especially rural land properties, through seller-financed deals and the uncertainty of how a buyer will behave on the land remains a very real risk.

From personal junkyards and scrap yards, to storing stolen vehicles and other criminal behavior, note buyers will do everything and anything on the property. These types of actions present a clear and present risk to the note seller.

Many years ago, my partner and I sold a property on a lease to purchase agreement. The buyer only paid about nine months of the fourteen-month obligation, and didn't complete the lease to purchase phase of the agreement.

As I was inspecting the property in order to resell it, I found many vehicles, boats, RVs, bikes, and other belongings left behind on the property — but two months later, those items had disappeared. Another client informed me that everything had been removed, but to this day I don't know what happened to it all, whether the items were his, somebody else's, or items stolen for scrap. One day they were there, and the next day they were not.

Soon after, my partner and I resold the property on a long-term land contract, and that client is still a reliable note payer, all these years later. Sometimes it takes a mistake to find the right clients. Real estate is not just about making money, it's about making sure people are treated right, and get what they want. As I've said before, if you don't provide for a client's needs, your competition will.

C. Uninvited guests: A third risk that sellers should be aware of is uninvited guests.

As a personal example, one of my longest term note payers (a client I had for ten-plus years) invited several convicted level-three sexual predators onto a property *after* my partner and I had forfeited him and his wife.

He and these uninvited criminal guests were occupying the property illegally. They were trespassing and knew it, but would not leave. I had a long discussion on the phone with the squatter's son, and said they all needed to leave as soon as possible. Shortly after, they finally left. We eventually leased the property to somebody new and never saw or heard from those people again.

Uninvited guests arriving during or after a foreclosure process is a very real risk for note sellers. Many times, the forfeited party doesn't care about behaving well or legally, as they know they've lost the property and have nothing to lose, and will bring these guests onto their property. It's one more obstinate act of rebellion against the rightful property owner.

To limit this risk, my advice is to have someone you trust to take physical possession of the property as soon as the foreclosed or forfeited party leaves. Make sure that nobody gets onto the property who doesn't legally belong there.

20. What are some tips for people who want to start a rural land note business and collect payments on a land contract?

Here are two great tips for first-time investors who want to build a rural land note business:

A. Start slow and learn as much as possible about the location of the property.

If you want to invest in and concentrate in a particular area, take time to learn as many statistical facts as possible about that area as you can. For example, how far is the driving commute from the property to the nearest city? As I mentioned in my first book, How to Make Money from Rural Land Property, most people are looking for rural properties that are within a thirty to sixty-minute drive to a small or medium sized city. And remember, there's a difference between a city of 30,000 people versus one with 100,000 people!

Long-term thinking means understanding the current trends while also considering future expansion. The analysis of a rural property's relationship to its closest city is wide, deep, and long — and another book could be written on just this topic. For example, you shouldn't discount properties just because they are a little further out, because the area might become more appealing (and the deals might be better) as suburban crawl expands outward over time.

B. If you want to buy rural land properties that are bordered or crossed by highways, expect a lot of local and peripheral development, disruption, and other changes in the area. Always consider access.

A secluded rural land property near a secondary highway can and does make a compelling investment. Access to a rural property is a very important ingredient in its total value. In my first book, I discuss land access in detail, and how it adds to the total value of an investment.

Access within, to, and around a rural land property located near a highway takes many forms. Many properties are close to highways, but developing a driveway or road can be tricky, complicated, and problematic. These types of things must be considered when purchasing rural land.

The very first property that I completely developed was on a highway. It wasn't a *well-traveled* highway, but a highway nevertheless, and I still like investing in rural properties close to or alongside highways. Some of my best investments have been directly on or very close to secondary highways.

21. What is 'water witching,' or what some call 'water dowsing'? Does it work? How effective is it?

Water witching or water dowsing consists of a person using two metal rods or two willow sticks to determine where well water can be drilled for on a property. Dowsing rods are said to give the person a better chance of finding a water source underground. Some well witchers (or dowsers) can determine the depth of the well, and roughly how many gallons per minute (GPM) can be produced by the well.

I've personally seen well witching pay off, resulting in huge water wells that I've paid to drill. Bringing a water witcher to a property of mine just north of Spokane, Washington, for example, produced excellent results. The wells on neighboring properties were a mix of good and bad, and I didn't want to take the chance of not having water. So before we drilled, the water witcher estimated a depth of seventy to ninety feet and a flow rate of ten-plus GPM for the water well. The actual well came out at eighty feet, with a fifteen-plus GPM flow rate.

On another property, a water witcher gave a conservative estimate for a well depth of 120 feet to 135 feet, with a flow rate of thirty-plus GPM. The team drilled the well at 120 feet, with a thirty-plus GPM!

It is imperative, however, that once a water witcher has indicated a water source, a big stake be placed in the ground in that exact same spot, so the well drillers know exactly where to drill. The type of well-drilling equipment used is also extremely important; it doesn't make much sense to have a good water witcher but use inferior well drilling equipment.

I learned this lesson the hard way. I once paid somebody to drill a well on one of my properties, but the cable ran out after 350 feet. There was more water at 385 feet, but the well driller didn't have the equipment to finish the well, and I paid $10,000 dollars for a dry hole.

In summary, water witching is extremely effective if it's done right. But make sure you have a well driller who can drill as far as needed, through hard substances, and around anything. You can read more information about wells in my earlier book.

22. What are the most common types of wells?

There are many kinds of wells, so I will try to simplify this question. Wells that produce 3 gallons per minute (GPM) or more can be divided into two groups, 'open face' or 'cased.'

A. 'Open face' wells are those that start with steel casing and are open at the end of the water source. These wells are usually found around granite or rock formations. In general, they're cheaper to drill because less steel is used than with other types of wells. The downside to an open well is that a good drill bit is needed to penetrate the granite or hard rock that usually surround them, in order to get to the water.

B. 'Cased' wells are those that have steel casing all the way from the start down to the water source. These wells tend to be found on properties with a lot of sand, gravel, clay, or other gritty formations. Most well drillers working in these conditions will place screens at the end of the well, as well.

In addition to open faced and cased wells, there are also natural artesian wells and other types of shallow water sources. I don't know much about these types of water sources, but if you have these, make sure to use water analysis and good filters to determine and maintain your water quality. Many times, shallow water sources can be contaminated.

23. What are the different kinds of septic systems, and what are some concerns to be aware of?

Some of the following information on septic systems is also included in my first book, How to Make Money from Rural Land Property.

Before we start discussing septic systems in detail, it's valuable to know that rural and semi-rural properties mainly use septic systems for sewage from mobile homes, stick-built homes, and any other structures on the land. In addition, creeks, wetlands, and any other water sources located on the property will affect your ability to install a septic system, along with other factors like the types of soil (loam, clay, granite, or sand), trees and plants present, and the slope of the property.

There are several ways to determine if a property will 'perc', which means that the land passes a percolation test and septic system installation will be allowed by a government official. A 'perc test' involves a process in which three to six holes are dug to determine the drain ability of the soil. These holes are usually four to eight feet wide, and six to twelve feet deep. Once the holes are dug, a local government official will test them by filling them with water and seeing how fast or slow the water drains.

In short, the speed at which the water drains from the holes will determine the type of septic system that needs to be installed. When a property cannot 'perc,' meaning that there's no possibility to install a septic system, the development potential and overall value of the property is usually diminished.

I've never purchased a property that could not perc. I like to purchase properties that can perc, and are able to be developed with septic systems. I'm not saying you should only do the same, but I'm a long-term rural land developer and investor. I want to, at some point (and usually early on), install septic systems on the properties I purchase, because more creates more. More septic systems mean more improvement, which means more people interested in a property. This higher demand translates into more income every month.

With all this in mind, here are 4 things to observe when buying or considering a property with no septic system:

1. Look for homes in the area near the property you want to buy. More existing homes usually means more septic systems installed.

2. Check with the County's health or planning departments and inquire about records of septic systems installed near the property you want to buy and develop.

3. Contact local septic installers and ask them what types of septic systems the County (or local government body) has been approving.

4. Get engineers involved who know the soil in the area and how it drains, and the type of septic system that will be needed if the perc becomes marginal, difficult, or impossible.

24. Do you have examples of note income generation and the techniques you used?

Yes. I have several:

A. This first example is from over nineteen years ago: My partner and I purchased ten acres, with power and phone on the property, with a transformer. In this specific instance, all that was needed to bring usable power to the property was one power pole and a service installation, which is a simple procedure done by a certified electrician.

We purchased the property for a little over $9,000 cash. The real estate agent didn't care about the property. In fact, he didn't even show me the property, despite being the listing agent. I drove out, looked at the property on my own, and bought it the next week. We cleaned it up, and sold it several times (via lease option) to several different people over the following years.

After a few years of having clients pay and then *not* pay regularly, we sold the land to a few local people in the same family on a lease option. After receiving payments for several years on the lease option, we converted the property to a real estate contract with seller financing.

As mentioned earlier, for many low or no down payment deals, it's better to start with a lease option agreement. If you don't know how to write this type of agreement up, consult with a knowledgeable person (another investor, a realtor, or a real estate lawyer) to help you.

The reason to start with these is because if a buyer quits paying, you won't have to forfeit or foreclose on the property. Forfeits (land contracts) and foreclosures (homes) get *expensive.* There's no closing on these agreements in the beginning, which is very critical to the long-term process, and the title doesn't transfer until the option period is finished and closed afterwards.

Most of the time, buyers walk away from the property. If they've occupied the property during the option period and refuse to leave after nonpayment, things get more complicated legally. That's why it's also good to have a disclaimer or restriction in the agreement about occupation of property.

In the example described above, the family members who purchased from us finished developing the property over time, and eventually placed a mobile home on the land. I assisted them with the septic system and well installation over the phone, and referred them to some of the people I'd worked with in the past. They did the rest, and to this day, there's a finished, developed property with a manufactured home on it.

My partner and I each receive a little over $180 every month on this property, and have been receiving these payments for the past fourteen years.

Although this is a simple example of selling a property on a land contract, all the parties involved in the transaction incurred some expenses and sacrifices, but in the end, everybody got further ahead before they started. Some utilities were there to start, but with more capital from the buyers, the property became fully developed.

We secured a good payer, who had skin in the game. We made the land payments affordable so that the buyers could use some of their money to continue to improve the property. We get cash flow every month, secured by an improved and more valuable property. And the buyers have an attachment to the property; people generate attachments to properties when they invest their own money and utilize their own time to make them more liveable, usable, functional, and, ultimately, more valuable.

B. My second example is from about fifteen years ago: My partner and I purchased a nine-acre property with two lots. Since I had experience with rural land highway property, I believed the property had good development potential.

Now, to help you understand what this means, I'll reiterate from my first book that 'development potential' represents one of the five criteria I use when evaluating a property to determine a good rural land investment from one that's not too good.

Development potential will swing a good investment to a bad one, and vice versa. And rural land highway property can be simple to assess (ease of access to utilities) and complicated to assess (time factor going forward) at the same time. You must consider specific highway issues (state highway concerns), security, and safety (small children running onto the highway, and cars crashing onto the property).

What's more, many end users and investors develop the home and surrounding improvements too close to the highway. When the highway and surrounding area is developed over time, through road enlargements and the associated easements, with more homes, and more of everything else (like utilities as fiber optic lines), the once-peaceful property suddenly looks, feels, and becomes something different.

In short, if one buys, develops, or improves rural land highway property, make sure a good amount of space, or 'frontage,' exists between the highway and the eventual homesite.

Which brings us back to the property in question — my partner and I did just that! Keeping 'frontage' and development potential in mind, we helped develop the property with the new buyers. The home was placed on the highest point of the property, at the expense of the buyers, with a good amount of highway frontage. This high point also helped facilitate the installation of a gravity septic system a few years later, which my partner and I paid to install with our team of experts. The well was also drilled away from the highway, where it was protected by other features as well.

The buyers assisted with drilling the well, and used their own money on the project. My partner and I helped them by referring them to a water witcher and well drillers. They hit a good amount of water, plenty for a few home sites. They also spent time and money running electric and phone underground to the home.

In a few short years, the property was fully developed and throwing off a few hundred dollars per month in income for me and my partner.

In most of my investments, I try to build long-term social and human capital with clients and this property was no exception. Still, the clients on this property decided to move, leaving the home and all the land improvements they'd made there. In time, somebody else bought the property from us, but he left as well, after only a short period of time.

At that point, we had one completely developed highway property and another that was only partially developed. A year or so later, we sold the developed property again, to a couple who now pays us just over $600 a month. We've now been receiving this amount for over ten years, and have sold the partially developed property, as well.

The lesson remains: Spend time with and help people who want to improve the property with their own time and money. Invest your own time and money as well. Good things happen in the present time and in the future. More improvements mean more payments, which translates to higher cash flow and more satisfied customers.

But this is not a fast process, as my example demonstrates. These improvements and agreements take time, patience, and trust. After many years and continued income, the hard work is worth it.

C. My third example demonstrates a longer-term approach to client building. With every real estate transaction, I try to think, act, react, and build toward long-term good customer relationships.

Over sixteen years ago, I purchased a property along a highway that had all the improvements, including an older mobile home and a garage with a concrete pad. What was different about this property from my usual purchases was that an older man and his elderly wife were already renting the property from the seller. After purchasing the property, I kept the tenants in place and maintained their previous leasing amount. The realtor who helped me with the sale knew the tenants, and I kept them on to manage the property.

A few years later, the man's wife died. He didn't want to continue living on such a big property and needed to find a new place. The realtor managing the property became my buyer's agent for a new property that I found in a neighboring town, which I recommended to my client. He looked at the property and bought it a few weeks later on a lease to purchase agreement, which was converted to a real estate contract a few years later.

Twelve years later, and I'm still receiving $550 a month from this client. I purchased the new property with 100% financing, and paid off the loan in fifty months. The point here is to remember to serve your clients today, and tomorrow if they need it. Serve your customers on a continuing basis, or somebody else will… And they'll become somebody else's client.

25. What is human and social capital in the context of the rural land note business, and how important is it?

A. 'Human capital' describes the tangible skills that people bring to the note business. These specific skills involve understanding numerical and financial data, familiarity with various contractual and legal agreements, negotiating acumen, and all-around relationships with people. These skills apply equally to realtors as well.

Many human capital skills are necessary to function well in the rural land note business. Some people excel well in certain areas, but they need help in other areas. When you have partners, employees, or associates in the business, these people can work together to ensure this skill set is represented.

As people stay in the business and gain years of experience, their skill sets get better. It takes time. It becomes a long game, like a baseball contest, where the game could be decided in the eighth or ninth inning. Sometimes it takes *years* to learn certain skills. Have patience with yourself and others around you.

B. Conversely, 'social capital' translates into your influence with others. Do you deliver what you promise? Do you have commitment? Social capital means how well people perceive, interpret, respect, remember, and ultimately admire you. It means how well you get things done. It means your reputation, along with the trust that goes with having a good reputation.

The third year I was in business, I had an interesting experience with social capital. I remember this example so well, even 20 years later. I sold a property on a lease to purchase agreement to a person who really admired and liked what I was doing. She trusted me.

She wanted me to meet her older brother, so that I could help the two of them start investing together, and to have the brother partner with me. What made this opportunity interesting was that he had received an inheritance and had money to invest in property.

Long story short, however, he declined to invest with me. I don't know what his reasons were. Maybe he thought I was too young, as he was a few years older than me. Maybe I didn't sell the dream good enough. Regardless, he declined, and I told him to call a few other people who could help him.

I wouldn't have invested with him even if he wanted me to, though. Not only had he been interviewing me, I was checking *him* out, to see if he was a good fit for me. He didn't seem to want to be in the game for decades, and I want to invest for life. I want to be and play the long game.

After that, his sister only made a total of ten lease option payments and I never heard from her again. Maybe they bought houses and flipped them. I don't know whatever happened to them. The rural land business is a long game. I think their time horizon was too short, and I'm glad I didn't partner with them. I sold the property to somebody else a few months later on another lease option.

Another time, a few years later, somebody who needed my help was referred to me. They told me that they only wanted to deal with me, and nobody else, so I drove over to help them out.

They invited me into their house, and I spoke with them, took care of them, and helped them with their land problems. I gave the deal to an agent I was working with, and didn't take any referral money. I wanted to build social capital instead.

Even though I didn't make any money from the interaction, I was able to help somebody out of a problem, which led to a more lucrative referral on another property a year later. Social capital is always critical in the rural land note business, because people in rural areas have a good sense of who is a shady versus legitimate investor.

Both human and social capital skills are needed to succeed in the rural land note business. Keep improving on both. Don't make excuses for your failures; learn from them and get better.

26. Compare and contrast flipping properties with selling on a long-term land contract. What is better? What should we consider in each circumstance?

To grow a business from a few good cash-flowing properties to multiple profitable properties, we should use every tool, technique, and skill available to us. Therefore, to build a bigger cash-flowing note portfolio that leads to consistent income generation, a combination of flipping properties and long-term land contracts works well if executed properly.

For example, over sixteen years ago, I bought, developed, and sold a property on a land contract. The property was very problematic and had many issues to deal with. I sold it to a client for a moderate down payment and land payments of $440 per month, and was cashed out of the property sixteen months later.

Next, I used the cash-out funds to buy another property with a mobile home attached, which had an existing tenant already in place. I received $500 per month in payments from the new tenant's land lease. When the tenant's wife died, he wanted to move, and I found him another property in an area that he liked better.

I sold him the other property and only a year or two later was receiving over $525 a month in payments. Eventually, I sold the property again, and for the past ten years have received $540 dollars per month, every month.

As you can see, I used the funds from the cash out to build a larger monthly payment income, with longer terms. I like cash outs, but the funds can dissipate without a game plan.

For me, I prefer long-term land contracts more than trying to buy and flip properties for quick gains. Flipping properties has been great for many people; they have their system, and it works. It's important to find a system that works for you and apply it. It will take time.

As far as which is better — to flip or to sell on a long-term land contract — all that matters is what works for the land investor making those choices, and the expectations they have, whether small or big.

27. List a few things that we all need to consider when working in the rural land note income business.

There must be a balance between running a business and having patience with people, their circumstances, and changes in society in general. This balance will be different for everyone.

Personally, I believe in having big picture objectives that are personal, professional, and tangible to me. We should never let a situation, client, or third party compromise our beliefs, standards, and personal safety.

Still, we must remain flexible. We need to listen more, speak less, and seek to understand *first*, instead of judging and criticizing others mentally and verbally. In addition, we must adapt and adjust as well. Crying, complaining, or having a personal pity party doesn't help us, the clients we serve, or their families.

I've learned a lot in my thirty years of experience in this field. But I'm still learning, and will be until I lapse in a coma, become mentally incompetent, or die. I will never believe or act as if I've 'arrived' or have figured everything out — and others shouldn't either. Yes, experience helps and it can reduce errors in many areas. However, many times newer experiences happen from a macro and micro level, and everything we know gets turned upside down.

For example, COVID-19 was one of those new experiences for everybody. There had been no previous experience of that magnitude, for anybody. Everybody, at some point, had to start over. We had to learn new things. We had to understand that some things were changing, and not the way we thought they would. 'Adjust and adapt' became the buzz words for many people. Uncertainty, fear, and anxiety created an unusual atmosphere in all areas of real estate. People did many things they would not have done, both positive and negative actions.

Despite this occurrence, the business of rural land note income continues. People who can't obtain financing at a bank still need that financing. Clients still need us to be patient when the payments are not arriving on time.

In fact, more patience is needed when buyers fall many months behind. Yes, some might follow an arbitrary three-month or six-month rule, and say that they will forfeit or foreclose after exactly three or six months of owing. But I don't follow any of those arbitrary timelines. If that system works for you, stay with what works, but I can't put clients on a timeline and make them act or not act a certain way. I'm a firm believer for timely payments like any other note investor, though, don't get me wrong.

When things get ugly, contempt rears its head. I've seen much of this over the last fifteen years, and have personally been on the receiving end of this contempt in many ways. Despite treating people well and giving them respect, the hand that helps will still get bit. Continuing to serve, help, and support people (including your clients) who have contempt for you and your business becomes one of the hardest things to do in life.

What can we do? We need to remember our purpose, our priorities, and most of all, the people we serve, including our clients and family. We need to remember that this note business has a multiplier effect; other people are positively affected by our actions, reactions, and inactions. We need to remember that at the end of the day, the month, and the year, memories will be created. Try to make as many positive, impactful memories as you can for yourself, your family, your partners, and for your clients.

Chapter Five

More things to consider

I started my business without a specific purpose, goal, or system. I didn't know anything about rural land property, not to mention developing, logging, improving, or financing it. Knowledge, experience, and the ability to apply that knowledge and experience took time to develop.

If you're reading this book and don't own any rural land property, don't be too concerned. I don't believe in rushing into anything that I don't know about, but I don't like to overthink things either. If you're experienced in the rural land business and have been doing things well for years, continue to do what works. Continue to look for feedback, and look to improve on what's already working. Don't stand still.

There's much to learn and know about rural land property. I've been involved in rural land property for over thirty years, twenty of which have been full time. I'm still learning, and will be until the day I die.

We're never too old or too experienced to learn new things about a subject we know well. There might be something that was overlooked for years, and nobody mentioned it to you. For example, many people will like nine out of ten things you do, but there's this one thing that they don't like. Understand, own it, and work on that one thing.

Here are a few more things to consider:

A. If you're a note seller on a rural land property, the affordability of your client's monthly payments is extremely important.

In my first book, How to Make Money from Rural Land Property, I mentioned the 'one percent rule.' This rule is based on a selling price, and states that you should rent or sell a property at one percent of its total cost. For example, if the market value of your property is $50,000, you should be able to get $500 dollars per month in payments. In addition, there are location considerations that will be specific to each property. It goes without saying, but I will say it here to be sure, that some places will rent or sell at a higher monthly payment than others. This is true statewide, and everywhere.

Keep in mind that this one percent analysis is only a general guide. Since the price of real estate has escalated very rapidly the past ten years and continues to do so, this guideline is hard to implement. I will say that no matter what price an investor pays for his property, they can only sell, lease, or rent it at a certain price before it becomes too expensive for the local population to afford. There is a price limit for everybody.

Making a monthly payment affordable, and at times *really* affordable (some might say leaving money on the table), ensures timely, long lasting, and satisfied purchasers. This helps you, the note seller, to build a business and create scale. This also reduces costly forfeiture actions, not to mention possible eviction procedures, if applicable.

B. If you're a buyer and are looking to sell the property on a loan to another person while maintaining another loan on the same property (called a wrap, or wrapping a bigger loan on to your loan), several things should be considered and investigated.

1. Check to be sure that your original loan does not have 'due on sale' or acceleration clauses on the loan.

2. If your original loan does have this type of clause, lease the property on a lease option for a few years to the person instead. Those proceeds will help pay off that loan before you close on the other loan, to avoid acceleration or due on sale clauses.

3. If no acceleration or due on sale clause exists, it still might be a good idea to start with a lease option for a few years, or to have a large down payment to pay off the first position loan, before closing on the next largest loan.

C. If you're a buyer and are uncertain of mineral right ownership, take the time for due diligence. I didn't really have an issue with this while investing in eastern Washington State, but in many other states this is a complicated and timely process. The same advice is true for timber rights. Not all rural land property conveys all rights, with everything attached or to be attached, and not everything can be determined by reading a title report.

D. If a property is landlocked with no legal access, try to obtain a legal and recordable road easement onto the property before closing. Or, more ideally, while writing up an agreement to purchase the property.

States each have different laws for addressing landlocked property. In Washington State, landlocked property is not allowed. I'm not sure about legal road easement laws in other states, but if in doubt, find good real estate lawyers to help you. Don't go it alone. And don't take a realtor's word on things, either. Most realtors are not practicing lawyers.

E. If you're looking to add partners to your business, or are in the process of partnering with other investors, make sure to identify and implement what each partner's role and responsibilities will be.

Many times, a person will partner with another only to find out sometime later that the combination does not work. The partnership becomes toxic, a negative in the short and long run for all parties involved. In fact, many times people's lives change for better or worse based on their partnerships. Partners get bored, lose focus, or get impatient with the results, including cash flow.

For example, I don't partner for very long with any investors or realtors who only want to flip properties. As I've said before, I don't flip properties. I like to keep and hold them for a long time. Having to buy, develop, and flip for a profit tends to burn through many people's pocketbooks and energy quickly. I've seen many people buy into the TV line of 'flip to wealth.' But these people forget to build a business model that's scalable, expandable, leverageable. They refused to learn execution, relationship building, and delayed gratification.

They usually don't last long. These types of investors often get into toxic and losing relationships with others, get taken advantaged, try to take advantage of others, and, many times, end up more broke than when they started. So a person who only wants to only flip a property will not work well with me and my long-term business model.

In addition, I don't partner with people who think they know it all or that they've arrived at some predefined goal. They are usually condescending, not teachable (how can they be, when they know it all to begin with?) and are an emotional drain of a distraction.

F. Lastly, my advice is to never partner with people who aren't able to trust you or your business model, or with someone you don't share a mutual trust of each other's skill set with, individually and collectively. I've encountered many people like this, and they have missed out on great opportunities for many things.

The rural real estate note business begins and ends with trust. The more someone trusts others, and shows the ability to be trusted, the greater the impact — not just for themself, but for others that are positively affected by this trusted behavior. Built-up, quality trust exists throughout short and long-term client relationships. It must never be taken for granted, or relaxed for even a minute.

Conclusion

Over thirty-six years ago, and before I started my rural land property note business, I was having a debate with some people about intentional (some might say expected) noise, and a lack of intentional noise. I remember it like it was yesterday.

The discussion centered around a hypothetical music concert. The question came up about some musicians and a conductor. In this hypothetical scenario, a conductor would show up, stand at the podium, and do *nothing* for five minutes.

The conductor would not waive their hands to start any music, or make any acknowledgement of the crowd. The conductor would then depart after five minutes, leaving everybody, including the musicians and the audience, surprised. The audience would not hear any music, only the noise of other people in the audience and the surrounding environment.

The question posed in this discussion: Was this a legitimate concert, with no real instruments being played? Or, if not, what exactly had happened?

After all, the audience paid good money to hear music. The musicians spent hours practicing their songs, but did not produce any sound from their instruments. The sounds the audience and the musicians heard seemed to be similar — the background noises made by each other, along with the outside noises of the community. It wasn't what was anticipated by either group.

Both the musicians and the audience seemed to have been short-changed by the conductor.

We can draw a parallel between this hypothetical situation and the real-life subject of the rural land note business: We look at property, expect to buy or sell a certain piece of rural land at a determined price, and hope to hear only what we want, and expect, to hear.

We, as buyers, expect the conductor — who in this example might be the seller, the realtor, or a client referral — to play our music, or, only entertain our wishes, price, or terms. And many times the conductor shows up and we *do* get what we expect, or think we do.

However, many times the conductor (the buyer, seller, realtor, or investor) doesn't show up the way we expect.

That's why it is always a good thing to have a Plan B or Plan C prepared for when things don't work out the way we think they should.

In today's world of much information, or I would like to call a 'concert,' there are many conductors. Some are legitimate, and some are not. In fact, it might be better that the fake ones stay quiet and don't do any conducting!

We can't get caught up in waiting for someone, something, or the next big idea to make us hear music (or to generate cash flow).

But it's also very important to listen — to attempt to hear the sounds that aren't spoken, or that don't appear obvious.

For example, listen to the local sounds of traffic or the general noises of the environment during the day and evening in the area you might want to invest in. This noise level will say a lot. Any realtor or seller will emphasize the positives while they show you the property. You won't be able to listen to the local noises effectively while they're there. Do that by yourself at another time, with no interference, including phones.

Listen to your client's needs, whether you are the buyer or the seller.

Listen to your client's expectations. Sometimes these expectations are realistic, and other times they're not, until some cooperation, coordination, and compromise is made by both parties.

Listen to the property — look, see, hear, and visualize the property's potential. You must be the conductor in this one. Yes, good advice helps. But, in the end, *you* must decide how to approach (conduct) it.

Listen to your gut, your heart, and your instincts. These are critical in many areas of the business.

You must be your own conductor (investor) in the rural land property note business. The musicians — your helpers, mentors, partners, and family — are there to make the sound. And your audience — of cash flow, positive referrals, appreciation, and legacy building — and you *will* have one, will applaud, or be disappointed.

Acknowledgements

I would like to thank Vladimir Verano from VertVolta Design in Seattle, Washington, for organizing, categorizing, and laying out the necessary information to complete this finished book. In addition, I thank Jessica Levey, my editor, for her excellent review, encouragement, and necessary corrections.

I would also like to thank all my past and current clients, who have trusted and continue to trust me with their rural property pursuits. If I had the chance to do it all over again, I would. I might change a few small things the second time around, but I would still be a willing participant.

I would like to thank all the real estate professionals that have helped me along the way over the past thirty-plus years. No man or woman is an island in the real estate profession, including the rural land note business, and no one can do everything themselves. It takes a team with different skill sets to win.

And lastly, I would like to thank many of the sailors I served with in my Naval career during my nine-plus years of service. The experience that I gained on three Navy ships has helped me with many things in my rural land note business. It wasn't all fun, excitement, and good times. It built discipline, persistence, and determination.

About the Author

Nicholas W. Maslaney started his rural real estate career in September of 1991 by buying 40 acres of property in Okanogan, Washington. Fifteen months later, he purchased another adjacent 40-acre property.

Since making these two purchases, Nicholas has bought and developed many different rural land properties over the course of a successful 30 year career, and has originated many loans on rural land properties.

Nicholas takes a long-term approach to his rural land property investments and note business. He prefers long-term land contracts, usually starting with option agreements.